Dilophosaurus
The Two-Crested Dinosaur

Dinosaur Books For Young Readers
By
Enrique Fiesta

Mendon Cottage Books

JD-Biz Publishing

Read More Amazing Animal Books

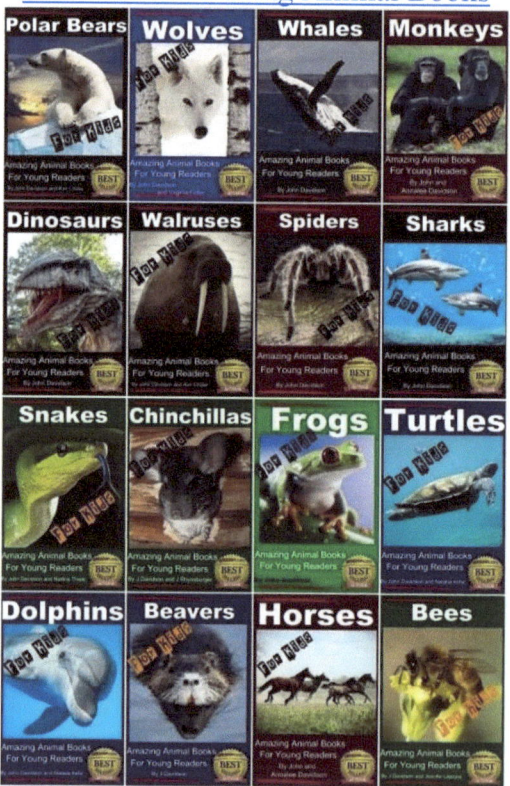

Purchase at Amazon.com

Table of Contents

Introduction

Hello young reader! Today we are going to go back in time to the age of the dinosaurs. The dinosaurs are an extinct species of animal that lived on the planet Earth millions of years ago. Extinct means that they no longer exist. They are some of the most intriguing, mysterious, and wonderful creatures to have existed on our planet. We are going to pay attention to one particular dinosaur in this book: the Dilophosaurus. The Dilophosaurus is an interesting dinosaur because of its strange appearance; it has two crests on top of its head. We are going to talk about not only the crests though, but about how it might have looked and acted and where it lived and what dinosaurs it lived with.

It is important that we talk about *why* we should even be talking about the dinosaurs- they are extinct after all. This, though, is a silly question! It is like asking why you should like rose bushes, fresh breezes, or anything else that isn't useful. Dinosaurs are *inherently* worthy of appreciation, just like rose bushes and fresh breezes. The study of dinosaurs also helps you to appreciate just how mysterious and amazing our planet is! Just think how cool it is that this planet could support life-forms as different as dinosaurs and human beings! The point is that one should approach the study of dinosaurs with a sense of wonder and openness, because dinosaurs are incredible creatures.

Chapter 1: Appearance

The Dilophosaurus is a cool and popular dinosaur because it has been used in movies and shows since 1992 (in 1992 the Dilophosaurus was given a cool design; it had frills and it could spit poison). The movies and shows do not often stay true to scientific fact, but they do keep the dinosaurs vivid in the public imagination. We are going to try to stay as close to the facts as possible, so that we can arrive at true knowledge. We will try to stick to what scientists believe to be credible. Scientists use the fossil record, biological data, chemistry, and other scientific methods to study and learn things about the dinosaurs. Fossils are the ancient remains of the dinosaurs. Most fossils that we get information from are the bones of the dinosaurs.

The Dilophosaurus was named for the two crests that protrude from the top of his head. "Di" is a Greek word for "two", "lophos" a Greek word for "crest", and "sauros" a Greek word for lizard. The name "Dilophosaurus" means "two-crested lizard."

The Dilophosaurus's two crests were rounded and made up of very soft bone material. This means that the crests could not have been used for anything save display purposes. If they were to be used for hunting, they would have to be significantly harder. For instance, the horns of the Carnotaurus were made of strong bones and some scientists think it used them to ram into other dinosaurs. The Dilophosaurus would risk breaking its crests if it tried a similar action. We will discuss what the Dilophosaurus might have used his crest for in Chapter 2.

The Dilophosaurus was a therapod. The therapods were a group of dinosaurs that were typically bipedal (walks on two feet as opposed to four) and carnivorous. They ranged from the size of small cats to as large as school buses. The Dilophosaurus was in between these two extremes as it could reach a length of 23 feet, a height of six feet, and weigh as much as 1,100 pounds.

Since the Dilophosaurus was a predator (an animal that hunts other animals for food) it was equipped with large claws and sharp teeth. It would use its teeth and claws in order to take down prey. Scientists believe the head of the Dilophosaurus looked similar to that of the modern day crocodile (in certain respects).

Scientists are unsure whether the Dilophosaurus was covered in scales or feathers and they are absolutely unsure as to what color the dinosaur (or any dinosaur) was. Some scientists believe the Dilophosaurus was covered in feathers based on a few fossils which have been discovered. The bones of the Dilophosaurus do not suggest feathers, but the fossilized earth underneath the dinosaur bear markings and imprints which have been interpreted as feather imprints. The fossil record tells us nothing about what color the dinosaurs were because we do not have any preserved skin fossils which have retained the dinosaur's original colors. The Dilophosaurus could have been green, brown, or tan like many modern day predators. This means that the dinosaur would have been camouflaged. Camouflage is a development in animals that enables them to blend in with their natural habitat. It is also possible that the Dilophosaurus was vibrantly colored like many modern day predators: the peacock, the tiger, and many lizards are very colorful predatory animals.

The color of the crests is also a debated issue. The crests could have been very colorful, much like the tail of a peacock. It might have born patterns which attracted prey. There are many turtles which use their tongue to catch prey- the tongue looks like a worm to the fish. The crests of the Dilophosaurus might have had patterns which prey would have mistaken for their own prey. In any case, it is a fun imaginative experience to look at the dinosaur from so many perspectives.

Chapter 2: Behavior

 The behavior of the Dilophosaurus was probably similar to that of most therapods. Since the Dilophosaurus was a predator it had to have spent a great deal of its time hunting prey. The Dilophosaurs, as we have discussed, possessed sharp claws and surprisingly long teeth.

Its crests were probably used to attract mates. This is why scientists believe the colors were most likely vibrant, because many animals today use bright colors to attract mates. Dilophosaurus males would compete against each other in order to win the favor of a female. The bigger and more colorful the crest, the more likely the male Dilophosaurus was to attracting a mate.

It is unknown whether the Dilophosaurus traveled in packs or was a social animal, but there is evidence for social behavior in the fossil record. In one circumstance, several individual Dilophosaurus fossils were found together. This group of fossils suggests that the Dilophosaurus may have been a pack hunter, much like modern day wolves. This is not necessarily the case, though, and more evidence is necessary to make any irrefutable conclusions.

There is a controversial claim, based on the fossils of the Dilophosaurus, that the dinosaur was not terrestrial, but aquatic. Terrestrial means "land-dwelling" and aquatic means "water-dwelling" when we are speaking about animals. The scientist who posed this theory claims that the skeleton of the Dilophosaurus is not strong enough to support its estimated weight (1,100 pounds). The scientist claims that the Dilophosaurus lived in shallow water much like a crocodile. It is important to note, though, that this is just a theory and that most scientists believe the Dilophosaurus was terrestrial. This theory has only been mentioned because it is an interesting take on the Dilophosaurus.

Dilophosaurus

Chapter 3: Environment

The Dilophosaurus lived in the Early Jurassic Period. The Jurassic Period is the second epoch of the dinosaur age. There are three: the Triassic, Jurassic, and Cretaceous. The dinosaurs ceased to exist after the Cretaceous Period due to an unknown cause. This cause is called the dinosaur extinction event. Some believe the dinosaurs were wiped out a meteor, a disease, climate change, or a combination of the three. Further research is necessary before a firm conclusion can be reached.

The Jurassic Period's environment was similar to that of a subtropical ecosystem. It was wet, drippy, and humid. Cyads, conifers, gingkoes, and tree ferns were dominant species. The Dilophosaurus would have to have been highly adapted in order to survive in this ecosystem. This is because it had to compete with many other dinosaurs for food and resources. Since the Dilophosaurus was a predator it had to have hunted other dinosaurs and small animals to survive.Here are a few of the dinosaurs that lived alongside the Dilophosaurus: the Anchisaurus, Scutellosaurus, and the pterosaur. The Dilophosaurus was the largest predator of the early Jurassic Period which makes it an apex predator. An apex predator is a predator that resides at the top of the food-chain in its ecosystem- the Dilophosaurus most likely had no natural predators.

The Anchisaurus was probably an herbivorous (plant-eating) dinosaur that walked bipedally. Scientists believe that this dinosaur was an early evolutionary predecessor of the sauropods (gigantic long-necked dinosaurs that walked on four legs). In the Early Jurassic, though, this predecessor of the behemoth sauropods was roughly the size of a large dog. This dinosaur was probably hunted by the Dilophosaurus because of its small size. The Dilophosaurus would have been able to easily kill the Anchisaurus because it most likely was unable to put up much of a fight.

The Scutellosaurus was a small, lightly-built, ground dwelling herbivore. It, like the Anchisaurus, reached the size of a large dog. One major difference between the two, though, is that the Scutellosaurus was covered in patches of armor. The Scutellosaurus was covered in what are called "scutes." A scute is a thicked, bony plate. If you want to visualize what they look like, think of the backs of crocodiles. The scutes protected the Scutellosaurus from attack. They were most likely a food source for Dilophosaurus but they must have more difficult to take down due to their amazing natural defence.

Pterosaurs are flying dinosaurs. The Pterosaurs originated in the Triassic Period and survived until the Cretaceous Period. They ranged in size much like modern day birds. A pterosaur that lived in the Jurassic was the Pterodactyl. The Pterodactyl could achieve a wing-span of four feet and was most likely omnivorous (ate anything) or piscivorous (predominately ate fish). It is possible that Dilophosaurus fed on pterosaurs; similar to how modern day cats feed on birds. The Dilophosaurus would have had to move slowly and silently in order to ambush a pterosaur before it could fly away. If the Dilophosaurus was able to live in water, it may even have waited for pterosaurs and other dinosaurs to drink before striking them unawares (like crocodiles).

Conclusion

We have stepped back in time to look at this dinosaur, where and when he lived, the dinosaurs he lived with, and what a journey it was! By using our imaginations and knowledge we can engage, wonder about, and appreciate the wonderful mystery of the dinosaurs. By learning about and appreciating what the dinosaurs were we come to appreciate our own present age and all the wonderful creatures that live today. We discover how varied and mysterious life really is- we look at animals today with special reverence and awe be. Make sure you keep thinking, learning, and imagining, and really make sure that you never lose your sense of wonder.

Author Bio

Enrique Fiesta

I was born in Southwest Florida and I hold a degree in Latin and Greek language and literature. In addition to my principal studies, I have also studied philosophy, history, the natural sciences, and literature. In my spare time I devote the vast majority of my time to reading, writing, praying, and walking. I am currently pursuing legal studies in order to become an attorney.

Our books are available at
1. Amazon.com
2. Barnes and Noble
3. Itunes
4. Kobo
5. Smashwords
6. Google Play Books

Bonus Dinosaur Content

Introduction to Dinosaurs

We will start our journey with dinosaurs with the Tyrannosaurus Rex. The fossilized remains of the Tyrannosaurus are found in the world's biggest dig sites, which are located in Montana. Palaeontologists discover new things about dinosaurs in dig sites. Dinosaurs can be huge, weird, tiny and even wonderful. The Tyrannosaurus Rex, as we will find out, was one of the huge dinosaurs palaeontologists have discovered.

Tyrannosaurus Rex

The word dinosaur is derived from the ancient Greek words "deinos" and "saurus." These words translated into English mean "terrible lizard." Dinosaurs were creatures who dwelled on Earth and dominated the life of this planet during the Mesozoic Era which was about 65 million years ago. There were also flying and marine dinosaurs and they existed with the land-dwelling dinosaurs for about 150 million years. Dinosaurs occupied every kind of environment and climate which existed on Earth at those times. They could be about as small as the size of chicken to being 100 feet long and weighing 100 tons. Dinosaurs were one of two types: one was called Ornithischia which means bird hipped, and the other Saurischia which means lizard hipped. Dinosaurs could either be herbivorous, carnivorous or omnivorous. These are long extinct animals- there are no more dinosaurs today.

Microraptor© *Michael Rosskothen - Fotolia.com*

Facts about Dinosaurs

Have you ever heard of Dinosaurs? What are they? Here are some important facts about them.

1. Dinosaurs are reptiles that lived on earth over 230 million years ago.

2. The word Dinosaur originated from Greek words "terrible lizard."

3. Dinosaurs are extinct and cannot be found on earth alive right now, but their fossils can be extracted for study.

4. The heaviest dinosaurs weighed about 80 tons, and they are called brachiosaurs. Brachiosaurs had a height of 16 meters and a length of 26 meters.

5. Dinosaurs laid eggs which can be found in many shapes and sizes. The smallest egg of a dinosaur ever found on earth is about 3 centimeters in length and a large one was about 30cm in length.

6. When dinosaur eggs become fossils they harden like rocks but maintain their structure.

7. Troodon was probably the most intelligent dinosaur. Its cranial capacity was equal to that of an average present day mammal. It had grasping hands and stereoscopic vision.

8. Ornithomiminds were the fastest dinosaurs. They were able to reach maximum speeds of 60 kilometers per hour.

Fight between Euoplocephalus tutus and Troodon formosus

9. The oldest dinosaur bones are found in Madagascar and they are around 230 million years old.

10. Micropachycephalosaurus is the longest name of a dinosaur and it means tiny thick headed lizard .It was discovered in China.

11. Thecodontosaurus Antiquus was the oldest dinosaur to be discovered in Britain .It was discovered in 1970 in a place near Bristol. It was 2.1 meters in length.

12. Up to the present over 700 species of dinosaurs have been discovered and named. Palaeontologists are carrying out more research with the aim of discovering more.

13.108 species of dinosaurs have been discovered in Britain alone.

14. Megalosaurus was the first dinosaur to be formerly named. It was named in 1824.

Dinosaur Extinction

The term extinction is used in biology to refer to the end of a species. Dinosaurs became extinct 65 million years ago at the end of the Cretaceous period. Since this took place many years ago, it is hard for scientists to find the reason that caused the dinosaurs to become extinct. Rocks and fossils are used by scientists to find out what caused the dinosaur extinction. However, there are some plausible explanations for what could have happened.

The explanations put forward include:

Volcanic eruptions
Volcanic eruption are one of the suggested reasons. According to this suggestion, there was a lot of volcanic activity that caused changes in the weather. The dinosaurs were not able to adapt to the weather changes and so they died.

Diseases
Diseases could also have caused the death of the dinosaurs. A disease could have spread rapidly and killed them.

The Ice age
The climate of the planet occasionally becomes colder. These cold-periods are called ice ages and they might have killed off the dinosaurs if they could not survive in the colder weather.

Asteroid impact

Scientists believe that a very big asteroid hit the earth during the age of the dinosaurs. An asteroid impact could have altered weather patterns and possibly lowered the temperature of the planet. This is because an asteroid impact would have ejected tons of dust particles into the sky which would have blocked sunlight. If the sun is blocked plants cannot survive, then herbivores cannot survive, and then carnivores cannot survive.

Combined reasons or Gradual extinction
It is possible that no one factor alone was responsible for the death of the dinosaurs, but possibly a combination of volcanic eruptions, asteroid collisions, and outbreak of disease.

Dinosaur Fossils

Dinosaurs are animals that existed thousands of years ago. They are of different sizes and colors. Some have wings and other appear in their own physical appearance. Dinosaur fossils have been found all over the world.

Dinosaur Fossil

Fossils are what is left of these great animals. The bones that they left behind have been turned into rock over time. Today scientists can study these great animals by finding the fossils they left behind.

Dinosaur Eggs

Dinosaur eggs have been found all over the world. Some of them are very similar to large ostrich eggs found today. They have been fossilized over time and that is why we can still find them today. They generally tend to have more symmetry and a rounder shape than modern bird eggs. Baby dinosaurs found in fossilized eggs can be studied to learn more about the nature of these wonderful animals.

Dinosaur Egg

Dinosaur Names

The following are common dinosaur names and their meanings. Most names are coined from Greek vocabulary, but some dinosaurs are named after their place where they were discovered.

1. Albertosaurus -"Lizard of Alberta" refers to the fact that it was discovered in
Alberta.

2. Allosaurus -"Strange Lizard" due to its unusual bone structures.

3. Apatosaurus-"Deceptive Lizard" because it had bones similar to another dinosaur's bones. The confusion caused by this fact made the discoverer call the dinosaur deceptive.

4. Baryonyx -"Heavy Claw" because the first fossil to be found was a claw, and because this dinosaur's hands have large claws.

5. Brontosaurus- "Thunder Beast"

6. Coelophysis -"Hollow form"

7. Cynognathus -"Dog jawed" , because it has a jaw like a dog.

8. Deinonychus -"Terrible claw", refers to the large claws on its feet.

9. Dilophosaurus -"Two-crested lizard" because of the protuberances on its head.

10. Dimetrodon -"Two size of teeth" because it has a set of large teeth and a set of small teeth.

11. Dimorphodon- "Two types of teeth" possessed two different types of teeth, which is noteworthy for a reptile.

12. Diplocaulus- "Double stalk."

13. Diplodocus -"Double beamed lizard."

14. Dolichorhynchops -"Long-nosed snout."

15. Dromaesaurus -"Running lizard."

16. Elasmosaurus -"Thin plated lizard."

17. Gallimimus -"Bird mimic" because this dinosaur looks like a bird.

18. Giganotosaurus-"Giant lizard of south" refers to the gigantic size of this dinosaur.

19. Hesperonis- "Regal western bird."

20. Ichthyosaurus -"Fish lizard" because this dinosaur lived in the ocean.

21. Iguanodon -"Iguana tooth" the tooth of this dinosaur resembled that of an iguana.

22. Kronosaurus- "Titan lizard" refers to this dinosaur's large size.

23. Liopleurodon -"Smooth-sided teeth."

24. Maiasaurus -"Good mother lizard."

25. Megalodon -"Big-toothed shark" because this shark has enormous teeth.

26. Mosasaurus- "Meuse lizard."

27. Nothosaurus - "False lizard."

28. Ornitholestes-"Bird robber."

29. Ornithomimus-"Bird mimic" because of its bird-like appearance.

30. Oviraptor- "Egg thief" because they were believed to be taking eggs of other animals.

31. Plesiosaurs -"Close to lizard."

32. Pliosaurs -"More lizards."

33. Protoceratops-"First horn face" because of its single horn.

34. Pteradactyl- "Winged-fingered lizard" because of its long fingers which seemed to form a wing.

35. Pteranodon -"Winged, without teeth" because this dinosaur has a toothless beak and wings.

36. Quetzacoatlus- was named after the Aztec god Quetzalcoatl.

37. Saltopus -"Jumping Foot", because the first fossil found of this dinosaur was a leaping foot.

38. Spinosaurus- "Thorn lizard" because of the paddle-like spines protruding from its back.

39. Stegosaurus- "Roofed lizard" because it had bones on the back.

40. Suchomimus -"Crocodile mimic" because it looks like a crocodile in appearance.

41. Triceratops -"Three-horned face" refers to the three horns protruding from this dinosaurs head.

42. Trilobites- "Three lobes" refers to the tripartite structure of this creature's body.

43. Troodon- "Wounding tooth" refers to the dinosaur's sharp teeth.

44. Tyrannosaurus Rex -"Tyrant lizard" because this dinosaur is terrible to behold.

45. Utahraptor- "Robber from Utah", this dinosaur was named after the
place it was first discovered.

46. Velociraptor- "Speedy robber."

47. Yangchuanosaurus -"Yanchuan Lizard" because it was discovered in Yangchua.

Dinosaur Diet

The diet of an average dinosaur consisted either of plants, meat, insects, or some combination of the above. The dinosaurs which ate plants exclusively are called herbivores which literally means "plant eater." These dinosaurs ate fruit, leaves, grass, and roots from the earth and from trees. These dinosaurs possessed blunt, interlocking teeth which allowed them to easily grind up their vegetable diet. Some of these dinosaurs would eat rocks to help them digest their meals. It is speculated that these dinosaurs ate a lot, drank a lot, and slept a lot.

Other dinosaurs were carnivores which literally means "meat eater." These dinosaurs are more famous than herbivores because they are commonly depicted as the antagonists in dinosaur movies: think Tyrannosaurus Rex. Carnivores would hunt other dinosaurs down and eat them in order to feet. If they were anything like modern day predators, their primary source of food was herbivorous dinosaurs.

Carnivores were built for speed and possessed sharp teeth and sharp talons. They would use their speed to catch their prey, their claws to grip the grey, and their teeth to kill their prey. Some of these predators lived in packs and they would hunt together in order to bring down large prey they would otherwise not be able to kill.

Omnivores were dinosaurs which ate meat, insects, and vegetation. Omnivore literally means "all-eater." These dinosaurs would generally eat whatever was commonly available and sometimes they were scavengers. Scavengers eat the remains of animals which were killed by carnivores. These dinosaurs were specially adapted because they could survive in environments where other dinosaurs would die. If an area lacked meat or vegetation, an omnivore would survive but a herbivore or carnivore would die because of lack of food.

Feathered Dinosaurs

Shandong Tianyu Museum's discovery of partial pieces of fossils suggest that certain dinosaurs had feathers. A small skeleton of a dinosaur discovered later proved that the museum was correct. The fossil possessed feathers. Now scientists are speculating that a large variety of dinosaurs possessed feathers and these discoveries back up scientist's claims that some dinosaurs evolved into modern-day birds. Many of these feathered fossils are being discovered in China. These feathered dinosaurs possessed very complex and unique teeth. They were pointed, sharp, and peculiarly large. The teeth in their back jaws were broad and flat. Their teeth seem to indicate that they were able to eat both meat and vegetation, thus making them omnivores.

Dilophosaurus

Plant Eating Dinosaurs

Herbivorous dinosaurs were well adapted to eating plants because of their teeth and long neck. Their teeth were built specially for grinding down plant matter, and some dinosaurs had long necks which allowed them to eat from the tops of trees. The following dinosaurs are common herbivorous dinosaurs.

1. Sauropodomorphs

They are also known as prosauropods. They consist of dinosaurs such as Plateosaurus ,Massopondylus, Lufengosaurus and Anchisaurus. They were able to feed on trees up to a height of 1.2 meters. They had well adapted teeth which were roughened and diamond shaped which allowed for easy tearing of vegetation. They had thick muscles at the gizzards that helped to break down the food.

2. Ornithischains

They had horny peak that was sharp and protruding out of the mouth for cropping plants. Teeth were adapted for tearing the picked plant food before swallowing. They had a fleshy cheek which covered parts of the side of their mouths. In this group there were dinosaurs such as lesothosaurus, Orodromes and the Scelosaurus.

3. Larger ornithopods

They included dinosaurs such as Ouranosaurus, Iguanodonand, Hadrosaurus. They had a beak which was sharp and broad for picking plant foods. They had interlocking teeth which allowed them to tear vegetation easily.

4. Larger ceratopians

They had extremely narrow beak which resembles that of a parrot. The beak was used to feed on vegetation by cutting the vegetation. They had more than one hundred teeth behind the beak; the teeth were interlocking for easy chewing of the plants picked. Psittacosaurus was a ceratopian.

The Weirdest Dinosaurs

Let's discuss a few of the weirdest dinosaurs known to humans.

Oviraptor- This dinosaur looked very similar to a modern day ostrich.
Oviraptor was weird in the sense that it already had bird like features before it became extinct.

Ouranosaurs- They had spines coming out of their backbone which means it had a sail on its back, or a large hump of flesh like a modern day camel. Since it was discovered in a desert, it is possible that it was a camel-like dinosaur.

Carnotaurus- Looked like a tiny Tyrannosaurs Rex. The Carnotaur had horns on its eyebrows and incredibly tiny arms.

Mamenchisaurus was herbivore but what made it weird was the length of its neck. It had an enormous 35-40 foot neck and not
surprisingly, it could never stretch it to full length upwards but had to carry it parallel to the ground.

The Deadliest Dinosaurs

Here are some of the deadliest dinosaurs. These dinosaurs were the lions, tigers, and bears of their time, only much, much larger.

1.Tyrannosaurus Rex
It had numerous strong and sharp teeth. This dinosaur was incredibly large and was probably the apex predator wherever it lived.

2. Utahraptor dinosaur
It had single curved claws which looked like a knife attached to its feet. These dinosaurs might have hunted in packs which made bringing down prey an easier task.

3 Jeholopterus
This dinosaur had sharp fangs. It is believed that the Jeholopterus made a living by sucking blood from other dinosaurs such as large sauropods (long-neck dinosaurs).

4. Kronosaurus
This is believed to have been bigger than the present great white shark. It possessed bigger teeth and a bigger jaw size. Think of a whale-sized shark coming after you.

5. Allosaurus
The Allosaurus was a fierce predator. This is proven by its very powerful jaws and sharp claws.

6. Sarcosuchus

This was the largest crocodile of the dinosaur age. Its length was double that of the largest crocodiles today and its weight was equal to 10 modern-day crocodiles. It had a long and powerful neck which allowed it to jump out of the water with lightning-quick speed.

7. Giganotosaurus

It had a weight of about 8 tons and three strong fingers on each of its hands. It was the largest predator that ever existed on earth. A full grown Gigantosaurus was probably able to bring down full-grown sauropods (long-neck dinosaurs).

Flying Dinosaurs

There are several species of dinosaurs which could fly or glide. Here are four of the flying dinosaurs that inhabited the earth millions of years ago.

Dimorphodon is one of the flying dinosaurs that existed during the age of reptiles. This type of dinosaur had two kinds of teeth and it was around 3.3 feet in length with a wing span of 4 feet. Due to its inability to stand and walk, this dinosaur spent a lot of time perched when not flying.

Dimorphodon

Rhamphorhynchus in another flying dinosaur that had short legs, a long tail that was made of ligaments, and a wing span of 3 feet in length. It had a narrow jaw with very sharp teeth and had a beak which it probably used to catch fish.

Rhamphorhynchus

The *Quetzalcoatlus* was discovered in North America and it is known to be one of the largest flying reptiles during the time dinosaurs were living on earth. Its wing span was 36 feet in length, and it had large eyes, a crested head, a very thin beak and its weight is speculated to have been around 300 pounds. The bones of this flying dinosaur were hollow which meant it could fly for very long distances.

Quetzalcoatlus

The *Pterodactyus* lived near water and its diet consisted of fish and other kinds of small animals. Its wing span was 20 to 30 inches.

Kinds of Dinosaurs

There were many different types of dinosaurs. Here is how scientists have classified them.

Dino Basics

A famous British scientist named Harry Seeley, in 1800's proposed a classification based on their hip structure. Seeley classified two major groups called Ornithischia (bird-hipped) and Saurischia (lizard-hipped). These two types were further broken down into sub groups as follows:

Ornithischia

Thyreophora: Also known as the armored dinosaurs, these dinosaurs were herbivores (plant eaters) and lived in the early Jurassic to the late Creaceous age. Thyrephora simply means "shield bearers" because these type of dinosaurs had armor, plates and horns. This group included Stegosaurus, Ankylosaurusand Nodosauus.

Ornithischia

Cerapods: These are typically horned or duck-billed dinosaurs Just like the Thyreophora, Cerapods were herbivores however, these dinosaurs has better teeth that helped them grind plants better. Cerapods were able to extract more nutrients from their food because of their more advanced jaws.

Saurischia

Theropods: The name means "beast feet." Typically, these dinosaurs moved on two legs and were carnivores (meat eaters). Some of these kinds of dinosaurs were also omnivores (ate both plants and meat). Theropods lived from the late Triassic period until the end of Cretaceous period. Scientists have also discovered that birds are the evolved-descendants of Theropods. While the scary looking and most popular ones in this category are the Tyrannosaurus Rex and Veliociraptor, there were also other dinosaurs like Spinosaurus, Deinonychus, Allosaurus, Carnotaurus,

Albertosaurus, Megalosaurus, Yangchuanosaurus and much more.

Sauropods: These lizard-footed type of dinosaurs walked on four legs and were enormous in size. They had long necks and tails, were huge in size and had comparatively small heads. Sauropods were herbivores and included Brachiosaurus, Diplodocus, Seismosaurus, Giraffatitan, and Apatosaurus.

The Biggest Dinosaurs

During the Jurassic period there were many heavy, gigantic dinosaurs that roamed all throughout the earth. Some of the biggest dinosaurs are listed below:

Liopleurodon - Liopleurodon looked similar to an orca and a shark, and it was the biggest pliosaur. It had a massive body, huge flippers, and a long thick jaw full of teeth. Palaeontologists say that this type of dinosaur weighed over 30 tons and could grow to a length of 50 feet.

Quetzalcoatlus - This type of dinosaur was also huge in size as it had a wingspan of 45 feet. This huge pterosaur has received its name from the winged Aztec god.

Spinosaurus - Spinosaurus was heavier than Tyrannosaurus Rex and it is believed that they were bigger in size too. It had a mouth that was similar to crocodile's mouth and it also had a skin flap that protruded from its back which resembled a sail. It is believed that the sail helped the dinosaur regulate its body temperature.

Argentinosaurus - As the name suggests, the fossils of this dinosaur was found in Argentina. It was among the biggest dinosaurs with weight of over 100 tons and height of up to 120 feet. A single spinal vertebra is four feet in diameter.

Argentinosaurus

The Smallest Dinosaurs

Fossils have helped palaeontologists discover the smallest dinosaurs that lived on earth. They are as follows: The Humming Bird - It may seem strange, but palaeontologists believe that dinosaurs did not become extinct completely but underwent evolution. Humming birds are believed to be the evolutionary descendants of dinosaurs that lived millions of years ago. It weighs as little as one-tenth of an ounce, and is considered to be the smallest dinosaur species that lives today.

Lariosaurus - With a total weight of about 20 pounds and a length of 2 feet, this dinosaur was the smallest aquatic dinosaur. It had a long pointed tail and a streamlined body. It usually lived in water but it also dwelt on land. It was similar to amphibians because it could live in both environments.

Pterosaurus - Pterosaurus had hollow bones and were lightly built. The pterosaurs were of different sizes but the smallest one was just a few inches long. This carnivorous dinosaur ate insects, crabs and fishes.

Microceratops - The microceratops was the smallest herbivorous dinosaur. It weighed 4 pounds and had a height of about a foot and a half.

Microaptor - The microaptors were the smallest carnivorous dinosaurs. They had a height of just 2 feet from head to tail. They were also known as "four-winged dinosaur" because they had feathers on their legs and arms. Their diet consisted only of insects.

Author Bio

Enrique Fiesta

I was born in Southwest Florida and I hold a degree in Latin and Greek language and literature. In addition to my principal studies, I have also studied philosophy, history, the natural sciences, and literature. In my spare time I devote the vast majority of my time to reading, writing, praying, and walking. I am currently pursuing legal studies in order to become an attorney. After I earn my law degree I intend to pursue a doctorate in philosophy, literature, and politics.

Our books are available at
1. Amazon.com
2. Barnes and Noble
3. Itunes
4. Kobo
5. Smashwords
6. Google Play Books

Publisher

JD-Biz Corp

P O Box 374

Mendon, Utah 84325

http://www.jd-biz.com/

Mendon Cottage Books

P O Box 374, Mendon Utah 84325

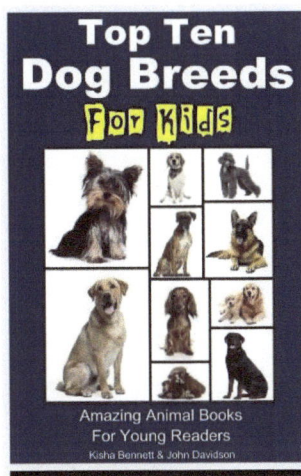

Top Ten Dog Breeds For Kids

Amazing Animal Books For Young Readers

Kisha Bennett & John Davidson

Poodles

Dog Books for Kids

K. Bennett

Labrador Retrievers

Dog Books for Kids

K. Bennett

German Shepherds

Dog Books for Kids

K. Bennett

Rottweilers

Dog Books for Kids

K. Bennett

Boxers

Dog Books for Kids

K. Bennett

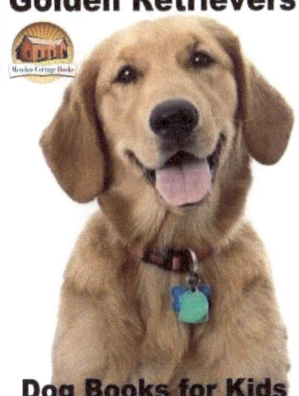

Golden Retrievers

Dog Books for Kids

K. Bennett

Beagles

Dog Books for Kids

K. Bennett

Yorkies

Dog Books for Kids

K. Bennett

www.ingramcontent.com/pod-product-compliance
Lightning Source LLC
Chambersburg PA
CBHW040746010626
45792CB00027B/281